MW00443083

CROCHET
Precious Baby Booties™

Designed by Carolyn Christmas

General Information

Many of the products used in this pattern book can be purchased from local craft, fabric and variety stores or from the Annie's Attic Needlecraft Catalog. If you need something special, ask your local store to contact the following companies:

Crochet yarn — **COATS & CLARK,** *P.O. Box 12229, Greenville, SC 29615*
Crochet yarn — **LION BRAND® YARN CO.,** *34 West 15th Street, New York, NY 10011, Phone (212) 243–8995*

Cross-Stitch Cuff Booties

FINISHED SIZE
Fits infant's 3½- to 4-inch sole

MATERIALS
❑ Red Heart Baby Sport Econo Traditional Art. E257 by Coats & Clark or sport yarn:
  2 oz. Baby Yellow #224
  1 oz. White #1
❑ 32 inches of ⅜-inch satin ribbon
❑ Tapestry needle
❑ G crochet hook or hook size needed to obtain gauge

GAUGE
4 sts = 1 inch; 4 sc rows = 1 inch; 2 hdc rows = ¾ inch.

BASIC STITCHES
Ch, sl st, sc, hdc, dc

SPECIAL STITCH
For **crossed stitch (cr st),** skip next st, dc in next st; working around dc just made, dc in skipped st.

NOTE
If a smaller Bootie is desired, use a size F hook. For an even tinier Bootie, use fingering or baby-weight yarn. For babies age 3–6 months, use size H hook.

BOOTIE (make 2)
Rnd 1: Starting at **sole,** with yellow, ch 10, sc in second ch from hook, sc in next 7 chs; for **toe,** 5 sc in last ch; working on opposite side of chs, sc in next 7 chs, 2 sc in last ch, join with sl st in first sc. *(22 sc made)*

Rnd 2: Ch 2 *(counts as first hdc),* hdc in same st, hdc in next 7 sts, 2 hdc in each of next 5 sts, hdc in next 7 sts, 2 hdc in each of last 2 sts, join with sl st in top of ch-2. *(30 hdc)*

Rnd 3: (Ch 2, hdc) in first st, hdc in next 12 sts, 2 hdc in each of next 3 sts, hdc in next 12 sts, 2 hdc in each of last 2 sts, join. *(36)*

Rnd 4: For **sides,** working this rnd in **back lps** only *(see Stitch Guide),* ch 1, sc in first st, sc in each st around, join with sl st in first sc. *(36 sc made)*

Rnds 5–6: Ch 1, sc in each st around, join.

Rnd 7: For **cuff,** ch 1, sc in first 10 sts; for **opening,** ch 6, skip next 16 sts; sc in last 10 sts, join. Pull up long lp to be picked up later. *(20 sc, 6 chs)*

Rnd 8: Join white with sl st in first st, ch 2 *(is not used or counted as a st),* dc in next 9 sts, dc in next 6 chs, dc in next 8 sts, dc last 2 sts tog, join with sl st in first dc. Pull up long lp to be picked up later. *(24 dc)*

Rnd 9: Pick up yellow from rnd before last, ch 3 *(counts as first dc);* working around ch-3 just made, dc in last st made on last rnd *(first cr st made),* **cr st** *(see Special Stitch)* around, join with sl st in top of ch-3. Fasten off. *(12 cr sts)*

Rnd 10: Pick up white from rnd before last, ch 1, sc in each st around, join with sl st in first sc. Fasten off.

Vamp
Row 1: Working in **back lps** only, join white with sc in sixth skipped st of rnd 6 at opening on Bootie, sc in next 5 sts leaving remaining sts unworked, turn. *(6 sc made)*

Rows 2–6: Ch 1, sc in each st across, turn. At end of last row, fasten off.

Sew Vamp to opening on Bootie, working through **back lps** only of skipped sts on rnd 6.

Cut ribbon in half. Center and weave ribbon through every two stitches of rnd 8 on Bootie cuff; tie into bow.❑❑

Colorful Booties

FINISHED SIZE
Fits infant's 3½- to 4-inch sole

MATERIALS
❑ Lion Brand Microspun Art. 910 by Lion Brand Yarn Co. or acrylic sport yarn:
    1 oz. Lavender #143
    1 oz. Turquoise #148
    1 oz. Lime #194
❑ 32 inches turquoise 2mm satin cord
❑ Tapestry needle
❑ G crochet hook or hook size needed to obtain gauge

GAUGE
4 sts = 1 inch; 4 sc rows = 1 inch; 2 hdc rows = ¾ inch.

BASIC STITCHES
Ch, sl st, sc, hdc

NOTE
If a smaller Bootie is desired, use a size F hook. For an even tinier Bootie, use fingering or baby-weight yarn. For babies age 3–6 months, use size H hook.

VAMP (make 2)
Rnd 1: With lavender, ch 4, sl st in first ch to form ring, ch 2, 11 hdc in ring, join with sl st in top of ch-2. Fasten off. *(12 hdc made)*

Rnd 2: Join lime with sl st in first st, (ch 2, hdc) in same st, 2 hdc in each st around, join. Fasten off. *(24)*

BOOTIE (make 2)
Rnd 1: Starting at **sole,** with lavender, ch 10, sc in second ch from hook, sc in next 7 chs; for **toe,** 5 sc in last ch; working on opposite side of chs, sc in next 7 chs, 2 sc in last ch, join with sl st in first sc. *(22 sc made)*

Rnd 2: Ch 2 *(counts as first hdc),* hdc in same st, hdc in next 7 sts, 2 hdc in each of next 5 sts, hdc in next 7 sts, 2 hdc in each of last 2 sts, join with sl st in top of ch-2. *(30 hdc)*

Rnd 3: (Ch 2, hdc) in first st, hdc in next 12 sts, 2 hdc in each of next 3 sts, hdc in next 12 sts, 2 hdc in each of last 2 sts, join. Fasten off. *(36)*

Rnd 4: For **sides,** working this rnd in **back lps** only *(see Stitch Guide),* join lime with sl st in first st, ch 2 *(counts as first hdc),* hdc in each st around, join with sl st in top of ch-2. Fasten off. *(36 hdc made)*

Rnd 5: Join turquoise with sl st in first st, ch 2, hdc in each st around, join. Fasten off.

Sew 17 sts of one Vamp to center 17 sts on rnd 5 at toe area of Bootie.

Cuff
Rnd 1: Working around top of Bootie, join lavender with sl st in first st of rnd 5, ch 2, hdc in each st around sides and remaining sts of Vamp, join with sl st in top of ch-2. Fasten off. *(26 hdc made)*

Rnd 2: Join lime with sl st in first st, ch 2, hdc in each st around, join. Fasten off.

Rnd 3: Join turquoise with sl st in first st, ch 2, hdc in each st around, join. Fasten off.

Cut cord in half. Center and weave ribbon through stitches of rnd 1 on Cuff; tie into bow. Knot each end to prevent fraying.❑❑

Icelandic Boots

FINISHED SIZE
Fits infant's 3½- to 4-inch sole

MATERIALS
- ❑ Red Heart Baby Sport Econo Traditional Art. E257 by Coats & Clark or sport yarn:
  - 2 oz. Baby Blue #802
  - 1 oz. each Baby Yellow #224 and White #1
- ❑ 32 inches of ⅜-inch satin ribbon
- ❑ Tapestry needle
- ❑ G crochet hook or hook size needed to obtain gauge

GAUGE
4 sts = 1 inches; 4 sc rows = 1 inches; 2 hdc rows = ¾ inch.

BASIC STITCHES
Ch, sl st, sc, hdc, dc

SPECIAL STITCHES
For **double crochet front post (dc fp,** *see Stitch Guide),* yo, insert hook from front to back around post of next st, yo, pull lp through, (yo, pull through 2 lps on hook) 2 times.

For **double crochet back post (dc bp),** yo, insert hook from back to front around post of next st, yo, pull lp through, (yo, pull through 2 lps on hook) 2 times.

For **popcorn (pc),** 5 dc in next st, drop lp from hook, insert hook in first st of 5-dc group, pull dropped lp through.

NOTE
If a smaller Boot is desired, use a size F hook. For an even tinier Boot, use fingering or baby-weight yarn. For babies age 3–6 months, use size H hook.

BOOT (make 2)
Rnd 1: Starting at **sole,** with blue, ch 10, sc in second ch from hook, sc in next 7 chs; for **toe,** 5 sc in last ch;

working on opposite side of chs, sc in next 7 chs, 2 sc in last ch, join with sl st in first sc. *(22 sc made)*

Rnd 2: Ch 2 *(counts as first hdc),* hdc in same st, hdc in next 7 sts, 2 hdc in each of next 5 sts, hdc in next 7 sts, 2 hdc in each of last 2 sts, join with sl st in top of ch-2. *(30 hdc)*

Rnd 3: (Ch 2, hdc) in first st, hdc in next 12 sts, 2 hdc in each of next 3 sts, hdc in next 12 sts, 2 hdc in each of last 2 sts, join. **Do not** fasten off. Pull up long lp to be picked up later. *(36)*

Rnd 4: For **sides,** working this rnd in **back lps** only *(see Stitch Guide),* join yellow with sc in first st, sc in each st around, join with sl st in first sc. Pull up long lp to be picked up later.

Rnd 5: Join white with sc in first st, sc in each st around, join. Pull up long lp to be picked up later.

Rnd 6: Pick up blue from 2 rnds before last, ch 1, sc in each st around, join. Pull up long lp to be picked up later.

Rnd 7: For **cuff,** pick up yellow from 2 rnds before last, ch 1, sc in first 10 sts; for **opening,** ch 6, skip next 16 sts; sc in last 10 sts, join. Pull up long lp to be picked up later. *(20 sc, 6 chs)*

Rnd 8: Pick up white from 2 rnds before last, ch 2 *(is not used or*

counted as a st),* dc in next 9 sts, dc in next 6 chs, dc in next 8 sts, dc last 2 sts tog, join with sl st in first dc. Pull up long lp to be picked up later. *(24 dc)*

Rnd 9: Pick up blue from 2 rnds before last, ch 1 *(does not count as a st),* **dc fp** *(see Special Stitches)* around each of first 2 sts, **dc bp** *(see Special Stitches)* around next st, (dc fp around each of next 2 sts, dc bp around next st) around, join with sl st in first fp. Pull up long lp to be picked up later.

Rnd 10: Pick up yellow from 2 rnds before last, ch 1, dc fp around each of first 2 fp, **pc** *(see Special Stitches)* in next bp, (dc fp around each of next 2 fp, pc in next bp) around, join. Fasten off.

Rnd 11: Pick up blue from 2 rnds before last, ch 1, dc fp around each of first 2 fp, sc in next pc, (dc fp around each of next 2 fp, sc in next pc) around, join. Fasten off.

Rnd 12: For **average ankle,** pick up white from 2 rnds before last, ch 1, sc in first 2 sts, skip next st, (sc in next 2 sts, skip next st) around, join with sl st in first sc. Fasten off. *(16)*

Rnd 12: For **chubby ankle,** pick up white from 2 rnds before last, ch 1, sc in each st around, join with sl st in first sc. Fasten off. *(24)*

Vamp
Row 1: Working in **back lps** only, join blue with sc in sixth skipped st of rnd 6 at opening on Boot, sc in next 5 sts leaving remaining sts unworked, turn. *(6 sc made)*

Rows 2–6: Ch 1, sc in each st across, turn. At end of last row, fasten off.

Sew Vamp to opening on Boot, working through **back lps** only of skipped sts on rnd 6.

Cut ribbon in half. Center and weave ribbon through every two stitches of rnd 5 on Boot cuff; tie into bow.❑❑

Ribbed Booties

FINISHED SIZE
Fits infant's 3½- to 4-inch sole

MATERIALS
- ❑ Red Heart Baby Sport Econo Traditional Art. E257 by Coats & Clark or sport yarn:
  2 oz. Baby Blue #802
  1 oz. White #1
- ❑ 32 inches of ⅜-inch satin ribbon
- ❑ Tapestry needle
- ❑ G crochet hook or hook size needed to obtain gauge

GAUGE
4 sts = 1 inch; 4 sc rows = 1 inch; 2 hdc rows = ¾ inch.

BASIC STITCHES
Ch, sl st, sc, hdc, dc

SPECIAL STITCHES
For **double crochet front post (dc fp,** *see Stitch Guide),* yo, insert hook from front to back around post of next st, yo, pull lp through, (yo, pull through 2 lps on hook) 2 times.

For **double crochet back post (dc bp),** yo, insert hook from back to front around post of next st, yo, pull lp through, (yo, pull through 2 lps on hook) 2 times.

NOTES
Wind a small ball of each color before beginning to be used for Instep.

If a smaller Bootie is desired, use a size F hook. For an even tinier Bootie, use fingering or baby-weight yarn. For babies age 3–6 months, use size H hook.

BOOTIE (make 2)
Rnd 1: Starting at **sole,** with blue, ch 10, sc in second ch from hook, sc in next 7 chs; for **toe,** 5 sc in last ch; working on opposite side of chs, sc in next 7 chs, 2 sc in last ch, join with sl st in first sc. *(22 sc made)*

Rnd 2: Ch 2 *(counts as first hdc),* hdc in same st, hdc in next 7 sts, 2 hdc in each of next 5 sts, hdc in next 7 sts, 2 hdc in each of last 2 sts, join with sl st in top of ch-2. *(30 hdc)*

Rnd 3: (Ch 2, hdc) in first st, hdc in next 12 sts, 2 hdc in each of next 3 sts, hdc in next 12 sts, 2 hdc in each of last 2 sts, join. **Do not** fasten off. Pull up long lp to be picked up later. *(36)*

Rnd 4: For **sides,** working this rnd in **back lps** only *(see Stitch Guide),* join white with sl st in first st, ch 3 *(counts as first dc),* dc in each st around, join with sl st in top of ch-3. Pull up long lp to be picked up later.

Rnd 5: Pick up blue from last rnd of Sole, ch 3, **dc fp** *(see Special Stitches)* around next st, **dc bp** *(see Special Stitches)* around next st, dc fp around next st, (dc bp around next st, dc fp around next st) around, join. Pull up long lp to be picked up later.

Row 6: For **vamp,** working in rows, using small ball of white, join with sl st in 16th st of rnd 5 *(will be a fp),* ch 3, (dc bp around next bp, dc fp around next fp) 2 times leaving remaining sts unworked, **do not turn or fasten off.** Pull up long lp to be picked up later. *(5 sts)*

Row 7: Join small ball of blue with sl st in first st, ch 3, (dc bp around next st, dc fp around next st) across, **turn.** Pull up long lp to be picked up later.

Row 8: Pick up white from row before last, ch 3, (dc bp around next st, dc fp around next st) across, **do not turn.** Pull up long lp to be picked up later.

Row 9: Pick up blue from row before last, ch 3, (dc bp around next st, dc fp around next st) across, **turn.** Fasten off.

Row 10: Pick up white from row before last, ch 3, (dc bp around next st, dc fp around next st) across, **do not turn.** Fasten off.
Sew ends of rows on vamp to five stitches on each side of rnd 5.

Rnd 11: Working in rnds, for **cuff,** join white with sl st in first skipped st on rnd 5 of Bootie, ch 3, (dc fp around next skipped fp, dc bp around next skipped bp) 4 times, dc fp around next skipped fp and around first fp of vamp at same time, dc bp around next bp, dc fp around next fp, dc bp around next bp, dc fp around last fp of vamp and around next skipped fp on rnd 5 at same time, (dc bp around next skipped bp, dc fp around next skipped fp) 5 times, join. Pull up long lp to be picked up later. *(24 sts made)*

Rnd 12: Pick up blue from rnd 5, ch 3, dc fp around next fp, (dc bp around next bp, dc fp around next fp) around, join. Pull up long lp to be picked up later.

Rnds 13–16: Pick up next color from rnd before last, ch 3, dc fp around next fp, (dc bp around next bp, dc fp around next fp) around, join. Pull up long lp to be picked up later. At end of last rnd, fasten off both colors.
Cut ribbon in half. Center and weave ribbon through stitches of rnd 11 on Bootie cuff; tie into bow.❑❑

Mary Jane's Slippers

FINISHED SIZE
Fits infant's 3½- to 4-inch sole

MATERIALS
- ❑ 2 oz. Lion Brand Cherry Red #113 Microspun Art. 910 by Lion Brand Yarn Co. or acrylic sport yarn
- ❑ Two black ½-inch shank buttons
- ❑ Sewing thread
- ❑ Sewing and tapestry needles
- ❑ G crochet hook or hook size needed to obtain gauge

GAUGE
4 sts = 1 inch; 4 sc rows = 1 inch; 2 hdc rows = ¾ inch.

BASIC STITCHES
Ch, sl st, sc, hdc, dc

NOTE
If a smaller Slipper is desired, use a size F hook. For an even tinier Slipper, use fingering or baby-weight yarn. For babies age 3–6

months, use size H hook.

SLIPPER (make 2)
Rnd 1: Starting at **sole,** ch 10, sc in second ch from hook, sc in next 7 chs; for **toe,** 5 sc in last ch; working on opposite side of chs, sc in next 7 chs, 2 sc in last ch, join with sl st in first sc. *(22 sc made)*

Rnd 2: Ch 2 *(counts as first hdc)*, hdc in same st, hdc in next 7 sts, 2 hdc in each of next 5 sts, hdc in next 7 sts, 2 hdc in each of last 2 sts, join with sl st in top of ch-2. *(30 hdc)*

Rnd 3: (Ch 2, hdc) in first st, hdc in next 12 sts, 2 hdc in each of next 3 sts, hdc in next 12 sts, 2 hdc in each of last 2 sts, join. *(36)*

Rnds 4–5: For **sides,** ch 2, hdc in each st around, join.

Rnd 6: Ch 2, hdc in next 11 sts, (dc next 2 sts tog) 6 times, hdc in last 12 sts, join. *(30 sts)*

Rnd 7: Ch 2, hdc in next 10 sts, (dc next 2 sts tog) 4 times, hdc in last 11 sts, join. Fasten off.

For **strap,** ch 15, hdc in third ch from hook *(ch-2 forms buttonhole)*, hdc in each ch across. Fasten off. Sew end of strap to two stitches on inside edge of Slipper. Sew button to outside edge of Slipper corresponding to buttonhole.❑❑

Sherbet Stripes Booties

FINISHED SIZE
Fits infant's 3½- to 4-inch sole

MATERIALS
- ❑ Red Heart Baby Sport Econo Traditional Art. E257 by Coats & Clark or sport yarn:
  - 1 oz. Baby Yellow #224
  - ½ oz. each Baby Pink #724 and White #1
- ❑ 32 inches white ⅜-inch sheer ribbon
- ❑ Tapestry needle
- ❑ G crochet hook or hook size needed to obtain gauge

GAUGE
4 sts = 1 inch; 4 sc rows = 1 inch; 2 hdc rows = ¾ inch.

BASIC STITCHES
Ch, sl st, sc, hdc, dc

NOTES
If a smaller Bootie is desired, use a size F hook. For an even tinier Bootie, use fingering or baby-weight yarn. For babies age 3–6

months, use size H hook.

BOOTIE (make 2)
Rnd 1: Starting at **sole,** with yellow, ch 10, sc in second ch from hook, sc in next 7 chs; for **toe,** 5 sc in last ch; working on opposite side of chs, sc in next 7 chs, 2 sc in last ch, join with sl st in first sc. *(22 sc made)*

Rnd 2: Ch 2 *(counts as first hdc)*, hdc in same st, hdc in next 7 sts, 2 hdc in each of next 5 sts, hdc in next 7 sts, 2 hdc in each of last 2 sts, join with sl st in top of ch-2. *(30 hdc)*

Rnd 3: (Ch 2, hdc) in first st, hdc in next 12 sts, 2 hdc in each of next 3 sts, hdc in next 12 sts, 2 hdc in each of last 2 sts, join. **Do not** fasten off, pull up long lp to be picked up later. *(36)*

Rnd 4: For **sides,** working this rnd

in **back lps** only (see Stitch Guide), join pink with sc in first st, sc in each st around, join with sl st in first sc. Pull up long lp to be picked up later.

Rnd 5: Join white with sc in first st, sc in each st around, join. Pull up long lp to be picked up later.

Rnd 6: Pick up yellow from 2 rnds before last, ch 1, sc in each st around, join. Pull up long lp to be picked up later.

Rnd 7: For **cuff,** pick up pink from 2 rnds before last, ch 1, sc in first 10 sts; for **opening,** ch 6, skip next 16 sts; sc in last 10 sts, join. Pull up long lp to be picked up later. (20 sc, 6 chs)

Rnd 8: Pick up white from 2 rnds before last, ch 2 (is not used or counted as a st), dc in next 9 sts, dc in next 6 chs, dc in next 8 sts, dc last 2 sts tog, join with sl st in first dc. Pull up long lp to be picked up later. (24 dc)

Rnd 9: Pick up yellow from 2 rnds before last, ch 1, sc in each st around, join with sl st in first sc. Fasten off.

Rnd 10: Pick up pink from 2 rnds before last, ch 1, sc in each st around, join with sl st in first sc. Fasten off.

Rnd 11: Pick up white from 2 rnds before last, ch 1, sc in first st; **picot, ch 3, sl st in third ch from hook;** skip next st, (sc in next st, picot, skip next st) around, join. Fasten off.

Vamp

Row 1: Working in **back lps** only, join pink with sc in sixth skipped st of rnd 6 on sides, sc in next 5 sts leaving remaining sts unworked, turn. Pull up long lp to be picked up later. (6 sc made)

Row 2: Join white with sc in first st, sc in each st across, turn. Pull up long lp to be picked up later.

Row 3: Join yellow with sc in first st, sc in each st across, turn. Pull up long lp to be picked up later.

Row 4: Pick up pink from 2 rows before last, ch 1, sc in each st across, turn. Fasten off.

Row 5: Pick up white from 2 rows before last, ch 1, sc in each st across, turn. Fasten off.

Row 6: Pick up yellow from 2 rows before last, ch 1, sc in each st across, turn. Fasten off.

Sew Vamp to opening on Bootie, working in **back lps** only on rnd 6 of sides.

Cut ribbon in half. Center and weave ribbon through every two stitches on rnd 8 of cuff; tie into bow.❏❏

Tap Dance Shoes

FINISHED SIZE
Fits infant's 3½- to 4-inch sole

MATERIALS
❏ Lion Brand Microspun Art. 910 by Lion Brand Yarn Co. or acrylic sport yarn:
  1 oz. White #100
  1 oz. Ebony #153 (black)
❏ 24 inches black and white ⅜-inch grosgrain ribbon
❏ G crochet hook or hook size needed to obtain gauge

GAUGE
4 sts = 1 inch; 4 sc rows = 1 inch; 2 hdc rows = ¾ inch.

BASIC STITCHES
Ch, sl st, sc, hdc, dc

NOTE
If a smaller Shoe is desired, use a size F hook. For an even tinier Shoe, use fingering or baby-weight yarn. For babies age 3–6 months, use size H hook.

SHOE (make 2)

Rnd 1: Starting at **sole,** with black, ch 10, sc in second ch from hook, sc in next 7 chs; for **toe,** 5 sc in last ch; working on opposite side of chs, sc in next 7 chs, 2 sc in last ch, join with sl st in first sc. (22 sc made)

Rnd 2: Ch 2 (counts as first hdc), hdc in same st, hdc in next 7 sts, 2 hdc in each of next 5 sts, hdc in next 7 sts, 2 hdc in each of last 2 sts, join with sl st in top of ch-2. (30 hdc)

Rnd 3: (Ch 2, hdc) in first st, hdc in next 12 sts, 2 hdc in each of next 3 sts, hdc in next 12 sts, 2 hdc in each of last 2 sts. (36) Fasten off.

Rnds 4–5: For **sides,** with white, ch 2, hdc in each st around, join.

Rnd 6: Ch 2, hdc in next 11 sts, (dc next 2 sts tog) 6 times, hdc in last 12 sts, join. (30 sts)

Rnd 7: Ch 2, hdc in next 10 sts, (dc next 2 sts tog) 4 times, hdc in last 11 sts, join. (26)

Rnd 8: Ch 1, sc in first 7 sts; for **ribbon loop,** ch 4; sc in next 12 sts; for **ribbon loop,** ch 4; sc in last 7 sts, join with sl st in first sc. Fasten off.

Cut ribbon in half. Insert ribbon through ribbon loop on each side of Shoe; tie into bow.❏❏

Fancy Sandals

FINISHED SIZE
Fits infant's 3½- to 4-inch sole

MATERIALS
- ❑ ½ oz. Lion Brand Mocha #124 (tan) Microspun Art. 910 by Lion Brand Yarn Co. or acrylic sport yarn
- ❑ Small amount Lion Brand Hot Pink #195 Fun Fur Art. 320 by Lion Brand Yarn Co. or novelty eyelash yarn
- ❑ 40 inches hot pink ⅜-inch satin ribbon
- ❑ Tapestry needle
- ❑ G crochet hook or hook size needed to obtain gauge

GAUGE
4 sts = 1 inch; 4 sc rows = 1 inch; 2 hdc rows = ¾ inch.

BASIC STITCHES
Ch, sl st, sc, hdc

NOTE
If a smaller Sandal is desired, use a size F hook. For an even tinier Sandal, use fingering or baby-weight yarn. For babies age 3–6

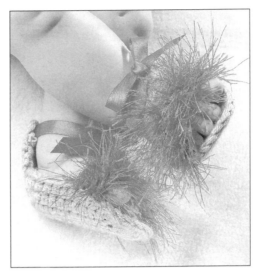

months, use size H hook.

SANDAL (make 2)
Sole
Rnd 1: With tan, ch 10, sc in second ch from hook, sc in next 7 chs; for **toe,** 5 sc in last ch *(for toe);* working on opposite side of chs, sc in next 7 chs, 2 sc in last ch, join with sl st in first sc. *(22 sc made)*

Rnd 2: Ch 2 *(counts as first hdc),* hdc in same st, hdc in next 7 sts, 2 hdc in each of next 5 sts, hdc in next 7 sts, 2 hdc in each of last 2 sts, join with sl st in top of ch-2. *(30 hdc)*

Rnd 3: (Ch 2, hdc) in first st, hdc in next 12 sts, 2 hdc in each of next 3 sts, hdc in next 12 sts, 2 hdc in each of last 2 sts, join, **turn.** *(36)*

Row 4: For **heel strap,** working in rows, ch 1, sc in first 3 sts leaving remaining sts unworked, turn. *(3 sc)*

Rows 5–7: Ch 1, sc in each st across, turn.

Row 8: For **ribbon loops,** ch 1, sc in first st, (ch 3, sc in next st) 2 times. Fasten off.

Vamp
Row 1: With eyelash yarn, ch 5, hdc in third ch from hook, hdc in each ch across, turn. *(4 hdc made)*

Rows 2–6: Ch 2, hdc in each st across, turn. At end of last row, fasten off.

Sew ends of Vamp to each side of Sole at a slight angle as shown in photo.

Cut ribbon in half. Insert ribbon through ribbon loops on back of heel strap leaving long ends to tie around baby's ankle.❑❑

Delicate Booties

FINISHED SIZE
Fits infant's 3½- to 4-inch sole

MATERIALS
- ❑ 2 oz. French Vanilla #098 Lion Brand Microspun Art. 910 by Lion Brand Yarn Co. or acrylic sport yarn
- ❑ 32 inches of ⅜-inch satin ribbon
- ❑ Tapestry needle
- ❑ G crochet hook or hook size needed to obtain gauge

GAUGE
4 sts = 1 inch; 4 sc rows = 1 inch; 2 hdc rows = ¾ inch.

BASIC STITCHES
Ch, sl st, sc, hdc

NOTE
If a smaller Bootie is desired, use a size F hook. For an even tinier Bootie, use fingering or baby-weight yarn. For babies age 3–6 months, use size H hook.

BOOTIE (make 2)
Cuff
Row 1: Ch 10, sc in second ch from hook, sc in each ch across, turn. *(9 sc made)*

Rows 2–23: Working these rows in **back lps** *(see Stitch Guide)* only,

ch 1, sc in each st across, turn. At end of last row, fasten off.

Sew first and last rows together for back seam.

Vamp
Row 1: Working in ends of rows on one edge of Cuff, skip first 9 rows from back seam, join with sc in end of next row, sc in end of next 5 rows leaving remaining rows unworked, turn. *(6 sc made)*

Rows 2–7: Ch 1, sc in each st across, turn. At end of last row, fasten off.

Sides
Rnd 1: Working in ends of rows and in sts, join with sc in back seam of Cuff, evenly space 35 more sc around, join with sl st in first sc. *(36 sc made)*

Rnds 2–3: Ch 2, hdc in each st around, join. At end of last row, fasten off.

Sole
Rnd 1: Ch 10, sc in second ch from hook, sc in next 7 chs; for **toe,** 5 sc in last ch; working on opposite side of chs, sc in next 7 chs, 2 sc in last ch, join with sl st in first sc. *(22 sc made)*

Rnd 2: Ch 2 *(counts as first hdc),* hdc in same st, hdc in next 7 sts, 2 hdc in each of next 5 sts, hdc in next 7 sts, 2 hdc in each of last 2 sts, join with sl st in top of ch-2. *(30 hdc)*

Rnd 3: (Ch 2, hdc) in first st, hdc in next 12 sts, 2 hdc in each of next 3 sts, hdc in next 12 sts, 2 hdc in each of last 2 sts, join. Fasten off. *(36)*

Holding last rnd of Sides and last rnd of Sole wrong sides together, matching sts, sew together through **back lps** only.

Cut ribbon in half. Center and weave ribbon through ends of rows at bottom of Cuff; tie into bow.❑❑

Lace Booties

FINISHED SIZE
Fits infant's 3½- to 4-inch sole

MATERIALS
- ❏ 2 oz. White #100 Lion Brand Microspun Art. 910 by Lion Brand Yarn Co. or acrylic sport yarn
- ❏ 32 inches white ⅜-inch sheer ribbon
- ❏ Tapestry needle
- ❏ G crochet hook or hook size needed to obtain gauge

GAUGE
4 sts = 1 inch; 4 sc rows = 1 inch; 2 hdc rows = ¾ inch.

BASIC STITCHES
Ch, sl st, sc, hdc

NOTE
If a smaller Bootie is desired, use a size F hook. For an even tinier Bootie, use fingering or baby-weight yarn. For babies age 3–6 months, use size H hook.

BOOTIE (make 2)
Rnd 1: Starting at **sole**, ch 10, sc in second ch from hook, sc in next 7 chs; for **toe**, 5 sc in last ch; working on opposite side of chs, sc in next 7 chs, 2 sc in last ch, join

with sl st in first sc. *(22 sc made)*

Rnd 2: Ch 2 *(counts as first hdc)*, hdc in same st, hdc in next 7 sts, 2 hdc in each of next 5 sts, hdc in next 7 sts, 2 hdc in each of last 2 sts, join with sl st in top of ch-2. *(30 hdc)*

Rnd 3: (Ch 2, hdc) in first st, hdc in next 12 sts, 2 hdc in each of next 3 sts, hdc in next 12 sts, 2 hdc in each of last 2 sts, join. *(36)*

Rnd 4: Working this rnd in **back lps** *(see Stitch Guide)* only; for **sides,** ch 2, hdc in each st around, join.

Rnd 5: Ch 2, hdc in each st around, join. Fasten off.

Row 6: For **vamp,** working in rows, skip first 15 sts, join with sl st in next st, ch 2, hdc in next 5 sts leaving remaining sts unworked, turn. *(6 hdc made)*

Rows 7–9: Ch 2, hdc in each st across, turn. At end of last row, fasten off.

Rnd 10: For **cuff,** working in rnds; join with sl st in first skipped st of rnd 5, ch 3 *(counts as first dc)*, dc in next 8 skipped sts, skip next 6 sts, dc in next 6 sts on vamp, skip next 6 sts on rnd 5, dc in last 9 skipped sts, join with sl st in top of ch-3. *(24 dc)*

Rnd 11: Ch 1, sc in first st, (ch 3, skip next st, sc in next st) around to last st, skip last st; to join, ch 1, hdc in first sc *(counts as a ch sp)*. *(12 ch sps)*

Rnd 12: Ch 1, sc around joining hdc, (ch 3, sc in next ch sp) around, join as before.

Rnd 13: Ch 1, sc around joining hdc, ch 3, (sc in next ch sp, ch 3) around, join with sl st in first sc. Fasten off.

Sew side edges of vamp to skipped stitches on rnd 5.

Cut ribbon in half. Center and weave ribbon through every two stitches of rnd 10 on cuff; tie into bow.❏❏

Pompom Booties

FINISHED SIZE
Fits infant's 3½- to 4-inch sole

MATERIALS
❑ 2 oz. Baby Pink #724 Red Heart Baby Sport Econo Traditional Art. E257 by Coats & Clark or sport yarn
❑ Tapestry needle
❑ G crochet hook or hook size needed to obtain gauge

GAUGE
4 sts = 1 inch; 4 sc rows = 1 inch; 2 hdc rows = ¾ inch.

BASIC STITCHES
Ch, sl st, sc, hdc, dc

NOTES
If a smaller Bootie is desired, use a size F hook. For an even tinier Bootie, use fingering or baby-weight yarn. For babies age 3–6 months, use size H hook.

BOOTIE (make 2)
Rnd 1: Starting at **sole,** ch 10, sc in second ch from hook, sc in next 7 chs; for **toe,** 5 sc in last ch; working on opposite side of chs, sc in next 7 chs, 2 sc in last ch, join with sl st in first sc. *(22 sc made)*

Rnd 2: Ch 2 *(counts as first hdc),* hdc in same st, hdc in next 7 sts, 2 hdc in each of next 5 sts, hdc in next 7

sts, 2 hdc in each of last 2 sts, join with sl st in top of ch-2. *(30 hdc)*

Rnd 3: (Ch 2, hdc) in first st, hdc in next 12 sts, 2 hdc in each of next 3 sts, hdc in next 12 sts, 2 hdc in each of last 2 sts, join. *(36)*

Rnds 4–5: For **sides,** working these rnds in **back lps** *(see Stitch Guide)* only, ch 2, hdc in each st around, join. At end of last rnd, fasten off.

Rnd 6: For **cuff,** working this rnd in **back lps,** join with sl st in first st, ch 2, hdc in next 9 sts; for **opening,** ch 6, skip next 16 sts; hdc in last 10 sts, join. *(20 hdc, 6 chs)*

Rnd 7: Ch 3 *(counts as first dc),* dc in each st and in each ch around, join with sl st in top of ch-3. *(26 dc)*

Rnd 8: Ch 1, sc in first st, skip next 2 sts, 5 dc in next st, skip next 2 sts, (sc in next st, skip next st, 5 dc in next st, skip next st) around, join with sl st in first sc. *(36 sts)*

Rnd 9: Ch 1, sc in first st, ch 1, skip next st, sc in next st; for **picot, ch 3, sl st in third ch from hook;** skip next st, sc in next st, ch 1, skip next st, (sc in next st, ch 1, skip next st, sc in next st, picot, skip next st, sc in next st, ch 1, skip next st) around, join. Fasten off.

Vamp
Row 1: Join with sl st in sixth skipped st of rnd 5 on sides, ch 2, hdc in next 5 sts leaving remaining sts unworked, turn. *(6 hdc made)*

Rows 2–4: Ch 2, hdc in each st across, turn. At end of last row, fasten off.

Sew Vamp to opening of Bootie.

For **drawstring,** ch 60. Fasten off. Center and weave drawstring through every two stitches of rnd 7 of Bootie.

For **pompom** *(make 2),* wrap yarn around three fingers 25 times. Slide loops off fingers, tie a separate strand of yarn tightly around middle of all lps, cut loops and trim to form 1-inch pompom.

Tie one pompom to each end of drawstring. Tie drawstring into a bow.❑❑

Ballet Slippers

FINISHED SIZE
Fits infant's 3½- to 4-inch sole

MATERIALS
- ❑ 2 oz. Lion Brand Peppermint Pink #101 Microspun Art. 910 by Lion Brand Yarn Co. or acrylic sport yarn
- ❑ 32 inches pink 2mm satin cord
- ❑ G crochet hook or hook size needed to obtain gauge

GAUGE
4 sts = 1 inch; 4 sc rows = 1 inch; 2 hdc rows = ¾ inch.

BASIC STITCHES
Ch, sl st, sc, hdc, dc

NOTE
If a smaller Slipper is desired, use a size F hook. For an even tinier Slipper, use fingering or baby-weight yarn. For babies age 3–6

months, use size H hook.

SLIPPER (make 2)
Rnd 1: Starting at **sole,** ch 10, sc in second ch from hook, sc in next 7 chs; for **toe,** 5 sc in last ch; work-ing on opposite side of chs, sc in next 7 chs, 2 sc in last ch, join with sl st in first sc. *(22 sc made)*

Rnd 2: Ch 2 *(counts as first hdc),* hdc in same st, hdc in next 7 sts, 2 hdc in each of next 5 sts, hdc in next 7 sts, 2 hdc in each of last 2 sts, join with sl st in top of ch-2. *(30 hdc)*

Rnd 3: (Ch 2, hdc) in first st, hdc in next 12 sts, 2 hdc in each of next 3 sts, hdc in next 12 sts, 2 hdc in each of last 2 sts, join. *(36)*

Rnds 4–5: For **sides,** ch 2, hdc in each st around, join.

Rnd 6: Ch 2, hdc in next 11 sts, (dc next 2 sts tog) 6 times, hdc in last 12 sts, join. *(30 sts)*

Rnd 7: Ch 1, sc in first 11 sts, (dc next 2 sts tog) 4 times, sc in last 11 sts, join with sl st in first sc. Fasten off.

Cut cord in half. Center and weave ribbon through stitches of last row and tie into bow.❑❑

1 Annie Lane
Big Sandy, TX 75755
© 2003 Annie's Attic

All rights reserved. This publication may not be reproduced in part or in whole without written permission from the publisher.

RETAIL STORES: If you would like to carry this pattern book or any other DRG publications, visit DRGwholesale.com

Every effort has been made to ensure that the instructions in this publication are complete and accurate. We cannot, however, take responsibility for human error, typographical mistakes or variations in individual work. Please visit AnniesCustomerCare.com to check for pattern updates.

ISBN: 978-1-931171-24-3   All rights reserved.   Printed in USA   16 17 18 19 20 21 22

StitchGuide.com

Stitch Guide

STANDARD ABBREVIATIONS

beg	beginning
ch, chs	chain, chains
dc	double crochet
dec	decrease
hdc	half double crochet
inc	increase
lp, lps	loop, loops
rnd, rnds	round, rounds
sc	single crochet
sl st	slip stitch
sp, sps	space, spaces
st, sts	stitch, stitches
tog	together
tr	treble crochet
yo	yarn over

sc next 2 sts tog......(insert hook in next st, yo, pull through st) 2 times, yo, pull through all 3 lps on hook.

hdc next 2 sts tog.....(yo, insert hook in next st, yo, pull through st) 2 times, yo, pull through all 5 lps on hook.

dc next 2 sts tog......(yo, insert hook in next st, yo, pull through 2 lps on hook) 2 times, yo, pull through all 3 lps on hook.

Front post stitch—fp: Back post stitch—bp: When working post st, insert hook from right to left around post of st on previous row.

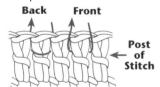

Chain—ch: Yo, pull through lp on hook.

Slip stitch—sl st: Insert hook in st, yo, pull through both lps on hook.

Single crochet—sc: Insert hook in st, yo, pull through st, yo, pull through both lps on hook.

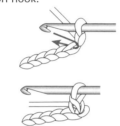

Front loop—front lp: Back loop—back lp:

Change colors: Drop first color; with second color, pull through last 2 lps of st.

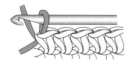

Half double crochet— hdc: Yo, insert hook in st, yo, pull through st, yo, pull through all 3 lps on hook.

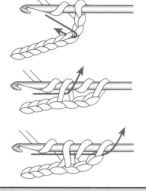

Double crochet—dc: Yo, insert hook in st, yo, pull through st, (yo, pull through 2 lps) 2 times.

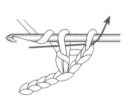

Treble crochet—tr: Yo 2 times, insert hook in st, yo, pull through st, (yo, pull through 2 lps) 3 times.

Double treble crochet— dtr: Yo 3 times, insert hook in st, yo, pull through st, (yo, pull through 2 lps) 4 times.

The patterns in this book are written using American crochet stitch terminology. For our international customers, hook sizes, stitches and yarn definitions should be converted as follows:

But, as with all patterns, test your gauge (tension) to be sure.

US		= UK
sl st (slip stitch)	=	sc (single crochet)
sc (single crochet)	=	dc (double crochet)
hdc (half double crochet)	=	htr (half treble crochet)
dc (double crochet)	=	tr (treble crochet)
tr (treble crochet)	=	dtr (double treble crochet)
dtr (double treble crochet)	=	ttr (triple treble crochet)
skip	=	miss

THREAD/YARNS

Bedspread Weight	=	No. 10 Cotton or Virtuoso
Sport Weight	=	4 Ply or thin DK
Worsted Weight	=	Thick DK or Aran

MEASUREMENTS

1 inch	=	2.54 cm
1 yd.	=	.9144 m
1 oz.	=	28.35 g

CROCHET HOOKS

Metric	US	Metric	US
.60mm	14	3.00mm	D/3
.75mm	12	3.50mm	E/4
1.00mm	10	4.00mm	F/5
1.50mm	6	4.50mm	G/6
1.75mm	5	5.00mm	H/8
2.00mm	B/1	5.50mm	I/9
2.50mm	C/2	6.00mm	J/10